REPORTINGS

ALSO BY TOM GANNON

Food for a Journey (2015)

REPORTINGS

Poems by

Tom Gannon

*To Kerry Temple and the
Notre Dame Magazine
staff — Keep up the
good work. All best
wishes —
Tom Gannon*

Antrim House
Bloomfield, Connecticut

Library of Congress Control Number: 2019952112

ISBN: 978-1-943826-64-3

First Edition, 2019

Printed & bound by Ingram Content Group

Book design by Rennie McQuilkin

Front cover art work and photograph by the author

Author photograph by Kate Gannon

Antrim House
860.217.0023
AntrimHouseBooks@gmail.com
www.AntrimHouseBooks.com
400 Seabury Dr., #5196, Bloomfield, CT 06002

*I dedicate this book
to Ann, to Mark and Sara,
to Kate and Devin,
and to the recently arrived Claire.*

ACKNOWLEDGMENTS

Most of these poems draw on my own experiences and on stories told me by family and friends. Several, however, required some research. For "Wars of Religion," I consulted Roger Crowley's *Empires of the Sea* on the maritime wars of the 16th century and a *New York Times* article on a contemporary incident in the Mediterranean Sea. For "Pilgrimage," I read Gordon A. Harrison's *Cross-Channel Attack* on the ordeal of 29th Division infantrymen at Omaha Beach on D-Day. For "Aspiration," I looked into John Marsh's learned discussion of the Prologue in the Pelican Commentary on the Gospel of Saint John. Finally, for "The Bump's Progress," I found that TheBump.com provided, for prospective parents (and grandparents), a marvelous metaphorical tour of a supermarket's produce department.

In my first volume of poetry, *Food for a Journey*, I tried to thank everyone who ever had anything to do with me putting words on paper. My gratitude to all of them endures, but several people have been especially supportive of my poetry since the publication of the earlier volume, and this is a good place to thank them. First in line are my wife Ann and my daughter Kate, who have been – Ann especially – the first readers and editors of the poems in this volume.

Next, I am grateful to everyone who arranged for me to read my poems before various audiences over the past couple of years: Jesse Cantrill of the South Bradley Hills Neighborhood Association; Miriam Kelty of the Bannockburn Community Association; Gennie Lalle and Patty Tobin, who invited me to participate in a poetry slam at Gonzaga College High School in D.C.; Abby Fennewald, the then events coordinator at Politics and Prose, the leading independent bookstore in the District; Sunil Freeman, the then assistant director of the Writer's Center in Bethesda; and Sara Daines and Marilyn Sklar of the Takoma Park Arts and Humanities Commission, who invited me to participate in a Third Thursday Poetry Reading at the Takoma Park Community Center.

Finally, I would like to thank the Canadian arts organization, Literary Excellence, Inc., for choosing *Food for a Journey* as a winner of its 2016 Book Excellence Award for Poetry. I'm particularly grateful for that honor.

TABLE OF CONTENTS

I. HERE AND THERE

II. DIAMOND MATTERS

III. ON THE WATER

IV. ON EDUCATION

I've always thought of myself as a reporter.

– Gwendolyn Brooks

REPORTINGS

I. HERE AND THERE

A Year's End

New Year's Eve, with midnight approaching,
Snow falling steadily out of the darkened sky.
The boy's parents out for the evening,
At a party with couples
They have known for decades,
Have shared this evening with
For almost as long.
His four siblings, all younger,
In bed and he hopes asleep.

He leaves the living room
Where the television shows
Images of Times Square,
The crowds roaring even before
The ball begins its descent.
He goes out to the glass-enclosed front porch,
Opens the front door and
With the night air cold upon his face
After the warmth of the living room,
He looks down the snow-covered rowhouse street,
So many of the porches ablaze through their windows
With Christmas lights, red and green,
Orange and blue and gold, not yet taken down.
He listens to the occasional snow-muted
Passage of traffic on the well-traveled avenue
At the end of the otherwise-silent street,
Tire chains clanking as
Vehicles churn through the snow.

He watches the snow falling softly,
The flakes drifting silently down,

Turning from gray to glittering white as
They enter a cone of light
From the house-high street lamp
A few doors down the street.

The peace and beauty of the snowy night
Strike him as something to be treasured,
Even as he is dimly aware that
In a day or two traffic on the street
Will churn the snow into slush and
The next rain will wash away the slush,
And it will be as though
The snow had never fallen so softly
Through the year-ending night at all.

At least, he thinks, he can cherish the memory.
Unlike the sight of the snow,
So lovely yet so fleeting
In the end-of-December darkness,
It will not disappear.

South Bronx Sunday

In the rectory dining room,
The priest who visits on alternate Sundays
Tucks into his bacon and eggs.
He has offered one Mass at nine,
Will offer another at eleven.
The pastor handles the ten in the upper church,
A curate the simultaneous Spanish Mass in the lower church.

The mood in the dining room is cheerful.
The nun who directs religious education classes
Has stopped by. The ushers
Who count the collection
Are having a cup of coffee before
Returning to their labors.

Then the housekeeper bursts into the dining room.
"There's trouble in the church," she says.
"We've called the police.
You people better get over there."
And they do, even though the visiting priest
Looks longingly at his half-eaten breakfast
As he rises from the table.

In the church, a strange scene.
The ten o'clock Mass is frozen in place.
The pastor stands stunned at the altar
Clad in green vestments,
Not in honor of Saint Patrick
But because the liturgical calendar
Demands green in what

The Church calls Ordinary Time,
But this is no ordinary time.

A man, small, roughly dressed,
Is striding up and down the aisles of the church.
In his hands he holds a six-foot length of
An automobile's muffler pipe,
And he uses the pipe to rap on the back of each pew
As he passes it.

The congregration is transfixed.
Everyone is watching the man with the muffler pipe,
Whose face is clouded with anger.
An usher approaches him warily,
Fearful of a blow from the pipe.
He addresses the man in English.
"What do you want?" he says.
The man shakes his head.
He has no English.
The usher poses the question in Spanish.
The man with the pipe responds in Spanish.
He is looking for a man, he says, an enemy.
Someone has told him that his enemy is in the church,
And so he has come to look for him.

The pastor has recovered from his shock.
Trailed by two altar boys, he leaves the altar,
Walks down the church's center aisle, and
Stops in front of the man with the muffler pipe.
"You need to leave," the pastor says.
"There is no enemy here, and besides,
This is a house of God."
The man with the pipe is not convinced.
He mutters his disbelief in Spanish.

Behind him, three of New York's Finest
Slip quietly into the church,
Begin to edge up the center aisle.
The pastor continues to converse
With the man with the pipe.
At length the police officers
Are close enough to pounce.
They wrestle the man to the stone floor,
Take away the pipe, throw it aside.
It clatters as it strikes the floor.
The man is handcuffed, hauled to his feet,
Walked to the back of the church and
Out into the street.
The police officers are breathing heavily.

The pastor, left alone now in the center aisle.
Looks around at the spectators,
The visiting priest, the religious education director,
The ushers, the congregation.
He shrugs his shoulders, lifts his hands,
Palms up, in mock helplessness.
"What can you do?" the gesture says.
"This is the Bronx."
He turns, retraces his steps to the altar.
The altar boys take their stations near him.
He finds his place in the missal,
And Mass resumes.

The visiting priest returns to the rectory dining room,
Silently mourning what once was his breakfast,
Thinking he should be more detached from worldly things.

Visitors

It began with two dogs
Barking excitedly inside our house,
Both rescued by our adult children,
Both ever alert to any unfamiliar activity
On the quiet suburban street
That runs past our home.

I went to a window, looked out, and
Saw three dapple-backed deer,
Two adults and a fawn
Quietly feeding on
Our next-door neighbors' lawn.

The tableau dissolved even as I watched,
The full-throated canine barking
Having had its effect.
The deer ended their feeding and
In their shyness, bolted
Across the black-topped street
Onto another lawn,
Then turned to the right and
Zigzagged with spindly-legged grace
Across more lawns until, finally,
At the end of the street,
Confronted with a traffic-heavy boulevard,
They turned again, left this time,
Around the curve of the last neighbors' lawn and
Disappeared behind their house.

Their graceful bounding summoned images of
Other deer-like creatures,

Gazelles and springboks and antelopes,
Sprinting for their lives, in flight
From big cats pursuing them across the African veldt
In *National Geographic* specials.

I had seen another deer too,
Watched it from afar as
It wandered to its death,
Seeking in its innocence
To cross six lanes of rush-hour traffic,
The deer crumpling on impact
With an oncoming SUV,
Dead on the spot,
Its legs splayed awkwardly
In the roadway.
No lions or leopards or cheetahs here,
Just lurking Toyotas and BMWs.

In their quiet feeding,
There had been about the deer on the lawn
A presence, an aura of peaceful calm.
I wished our dogs had stopped their barking.
I wished our visitors had stayed a while longer.
I was sorry to see them go.

Furiously Pedaling

He drives north in the curb lane.
She bikes south on the sidewalk.
They will pass yards apart
Moving in opposite directions.

She is lean of face and body,
Dark of hair, grim of visage.
She pedals furiously
In the cool of the morning,
And as she pedals,
The breeze lifts the tail of her sweater
So that it streams out behind her.

The motorist realizes
He has seen this scene before.
The images multiply –
The furiously pedaling Almira Gulch,
The broomstick-mounted
Wicked Witch of the West.

The cyclist passes the motorist now,
Her face still taut with determination,
In pursuit of her own ruby slippers.

Suburban Morning

He lifts himself on an elbow,
Peers bleary-eyed at the clock-radio
On the bedside table.
The numbers glow a bright electronic green
In the semi-darkness,
Say five-fifteen.
Too early to get up, he thinks,
And lies back, relaxing,
Crosses his hands corpse-like
Across his chest and listens
Through a cracked-open window
To the sounds of the world beyond.

He hears the birds first,
Three species, maybe four,
Each with its own distinct call.
He cannot identify most of them;
A birder would know,
But he is no birder.
He recognizes only one by its call,
The mourning dove, known by its plaintive cry,
The reference books say, and
He counts in his head
The four beats of its cooing.

He hears the sirens too, from multiple vehicles,
Police cruisers, fire engines, ambulances
Dispatched from the local precinct,
Fire station, rescue squad.
One siren is a high keening wail,

Another a canine wow-wow-wow,
A third sounds a harsh klaxon
Like a tugboat in a fog-filled harbor.
They mean trouble for someone, those sirens,
The victim of an auto accident or a violent crime, or
An elderly woman with a clogged artery
Who wakes to feel an elephant sitting on her chest.

He can see in his mind's eye the ambulances,
Imagines three of them, big, white, boxy Freightliners
Filling the ER's parking bays at a nearby hospital,
A busy day, starting early.

He has been a patient at that hospital,
Been treated in its ER and its ICU.
He can hear again
The early morning announcements
Over the public address system,
Announcements that someone is in real trouble:
"Your attention, please. Trauma Team One, incoming,
Code Two, by land, ETA five minutes."

Then it is six in the morning,
And with the coming of that hour,
He hears the first of the jetliners,
The throbbing roar of their engines overhead
As the planes climb for altitude
In their early morning ritual,
Heading northwest out of National Airport,
Over Washington suburbs like Bethesda and
Rockville and Gaithersburg,
On their way to Pittsburgh and Cleveland,
Detroit and Chicago.

He does not know their destinations,
But he knows they are somewhere to the northwest,
For he has seen their running lights,
Blinking yellow and white from
Beneath their bellies and wings,
As they rose in the air
From lower left to upper right
Through the darkness, across the blue-black sky
While he walked to the front edge of the lawn
And bent to pick up the morning's papers
Lying flat on the dew-wet grass
In their thin plastic sleeves.

He still lies abed, still corpse-like,
Hands crossed lightly on his chest
As the pre-dawn half-light
Seeps in from outside.

The birds twitter, the sirens wail,
The jet engines roar, and
He listens in silence
With attention and gratitude
And yes, some dismay,
To the sounds that give shape
To his twilit morning world.

II. DIAMOND MATTERS

Autograph

The brothers are eight going on nine and
Six going on seven.
On a cloudy mid-July morning
They are playing half-ball –
An intact pimple ball sacrificed
To the demands of the game,
A broomstick for a bat –
In the junior high schoolyard
At the end of the block from their rowhouse home,
The school named for literary effect
After Edgar Allan Poe.

A summons from their mother,
Calling down the street
From their front doorway,
Her high-pitched "Yoo-hoo"
Making the older brother cringe.

Back at their house
The boys receive their instructions:
"Wash your face and hands, and
Put on clean T-shirts,
A car is coming from Ford's
To take you in town.
You're going to meet Babe Ruth."

It is 1947, and Ford Motor Company,
Where the boys' father has worked
For almost two decades,
Is sponsoring American Legion Baseball,
And has engaged the Bambino,
The Sultan of Swat, to help promote the effort.

The car, the largest sedan Ford makes,
Arrives at the boys' front door.
They are placed in the back seat,
Minor celebrities for a few hours, and
Transported to the city's fanciest hotel,
Where they have never been before.

In a curtained conference room,
The brothers and six other boys,
Sons of Ford employees too,
Meet the Babe, a huge man
(or so it seems to the boys),
Not merely tanned but bronzed,
With broad familiar features and
A head of thick black hair,
Dressed in a double-breasted blue blazer and
A wide-collared, open-necked white sport shirt.
A handshake for each boy,
Their hands disappearing
In the Babe's massive paw.

The boys each receive a major league baseball
And are grouped around the Babe,
Each holding out his baseball,
Watching as the Babe takes one of the balls
And with the ball and a long cigar in his left hand
And a ballpoint pen in his right,
Proceeds to autograph the ball in blue ink
In his large, bold, unmistakable signature,
One of the world's most famous,
One that, like John Hancock's,
People can read without their glasses.

A photographer records the tableau and
Prints of the scene will soon arrive at the boys' homes.

The balls go home with them from the hotel,
To be enshrined in places of honor
Atop mantelpieces and bedroom bureaus.

A year later, maybe two, the older brother
Takes his ball to a tryout camp
Where a major league scout is evaluating
High school athletes for their professional promise.
The boy thinks to enhance the value of the ball
By adding another major-league signature to it,
But when he presents the ball to the scout for signing,
The scout hesitates, his instinct to decline,
To preserve on the ball the great man's signature
In all its pristine majesty.
What business is it of his, he asks himself,
To add his name to a ball bearing
The signature of the greatest player
Who ever lived?
He is but a lowly scout scouring
The fringes of organized baseball
For talented seventeen-year-olds.
But the older brother persists, and
Rather than disappoint him,
The scout signs, in tiny, cramped writing,
On the other side of the ball from the Babe.

After another few years pass,
It occurs to the older brother, now in his teens,
That there are things in his life
That he has not treasured as he should have,
That by adding the scout's autograph
To the ball the Babe signed,
He has devalued the ball.
He comes to realize that
Sometimes more is less.

More years pass, the older brother grows up,
Leaves home for college, and one summer,
When he comes home from school,
He can no longer find the Babe Ruth baseball.
He mourns its loss, but he consoles himself
With the knowledge that he still possesses
That photo from 1947, the eight little boys
Gathered around the great man.

Many more years later, the photo,
Framed now, preserved under glass,
Perches prominently on a bookcase shelf
In the older brother's living room.
He has not yet lit a candle
In front of that photo,
But someday he may.

Midget Southpaw

The father had little time
To take his sons to big-league ballgames –
A full-time job with a car company,
A shoe store job two nights a week and
All day Saturday, the job a favor from
A boyhood friend who managed the store –
All to make ends meet for
A wife and five children
Aged two to thirteen.
But there were exceptions, and
A hot muggy night in
August of Nineteen Fifty-Two
Was one of them.

The Athletics, the A's, were playing.
While seldom blessed with great pitching –
Lefty Grove a distant memory,
Catfish Hunter decades in the future and
A continent away –
This year they had a good one,
Bobby Shantz, "the midget southpaw,"
All of five foot six inches tall,
All one hundred and thirty-eight pounds of him,
The size of your average batboy,
Twenty-six years old, earning a princely
Twelve thousand dollars a year.
In early July, he had pitched
An inning in the All-Star Game and
Relying on his sidearm delivery,
Sharp curve, knuckleball, and
Firm control of the strike zone,

Struck out three redoubtable National Leaguers,
Whitey Lockman of the Giants (looking),
Jackie Robinson of the Dodgers (swinging),
Stan Musial of the Cardinals (looking).

Now, a month later,
With the Red Sox in town and
Nineteen wins behind him,
He was reaching for
Win Number Twenty.

The father thought that his two oldest boys,
Thirteen and eleven,
Would someday appreciate their chance
To watch baseball history in the making.

Off they went, the three of them,
By bus and subway and foot,
To the old ballpark
At Twenty-First and Lehigh,
To seats in the lower deck
Along the first base line
Where they had an excellent view of
A wickedly top-spun double by Ferris Fain,
The A's all-star first baseman and
Future batting champion,
As it skirled past first base
Into foul territory and
Skittered into the right field corner,
Igniting the A's offense.
As the game progressed,
That offense would accumulate five runs.

The midget southpaw was not at
His Most Valuable Player best that night:

Two names from Boston baseball history,
Hoot Evers and Sammy White,
Solved his left-handed offerings,
Lofted home runs into the
Upper deck in left field,
But the Sox managed only one more run.

Still, in the top of the eighth,
A moment of high drama.
The game still within Boston's reach,
Only two runs behind,
A familiar figure emerged from
The Red Sox dugout to pinch-hit.
Past his prime,
His four-oh-six average
Eleven years in the past,
But still a batter to strike fear
In the hearts of opposing pitchers.
Theodore Samuel Williams,
"The Kid," "The Thumper,"
"The Splendid Splinter."

The thirteen-year-old's recall of
That August night is not complete.
But his memory of the Williams at-bat
Remains strong. He still sees
The lanky man wearing Number Nine
Climbing out of the dugout,
Swinging two bats in the on-deck circle,
Tossing one aside, striding to the plate
Amid the mingling of cheers and boos
Reserved for opposing superstars.

A famed observer of pitched baseballs,
Williams took one pitch – or was it two?

No matter. He liked one enough to swing.
Thirty-five thousand fans
Paused in their breathing
As the ball rose high into the August night
In a majestic parabola towards the right field fence.

The suspense was mercifully brief.
The ball fell softly through the warm summer air and
Nestled in the glove of the A's rightfielder,
Six feet short of the fence and
Three feet outside the foul line.
Thirty-five thousand faithful breathed again.
The Splendid Splinter had fouled out.

A handful of Boston outs more and
The A's, so often so lowly,
Had a twenty-game winner in
The midget southpaw.

The trip home, on foot, by subway and bus,
Was euphoric, suffused with the joy that
Accompanies an historic home team win.

"You'll remember tonight for a long time,"
The father said to his sons.
Indeed they would.

A Really Good Set of Notes

In the early fall of the year,
A campus-wide invitation
Sent out by the brain coach,
The veteran college administrator
Charged with keeping the athletes eligible.
He called for prospective tutors
To guide freshman athletes
Through a survey course
In the College of Arts and Letters,
On the history of Western Europe.

The sophomore decided to volunteer.
He had aced that course the year before,
Compiling along the way a really good set of notes.
Besides, he could use the modest stipend
The tutors were paid.

He duly submitted his name to the brain coach,
Was accepted into the tutoring program, and
Was soon assigned his first freshman pupil,
A burly young man, a walk-on linebacker,
A serious student who came faithfully
To the tutoring sessions, but grew so discouraged
Over his gridiron prospects –
A half-dozen scholarship athletes
Ahead of him on the depth chart –
That he decided to transfer at the semester's end and
Dropped out of the tutoring program.

The tutor's next project,
A much-recruited scholarship center and linebacker

With an impressive resume that included
All-state honors back in the East,
Turned out to suffer from
A severe, ultimately self-destructive case
Of athletic entitlement.
He could not be bothered to open
The textbook his scholarship had paid for,
And found one spurious reason after another
To absent himself from the tutoring sessions.

The tutor notified the brain coach,
Who told him not to worry:
The athlete's association with the university
Was unlikely to last much longer.
The brain coach was prescient.
After a drunken episode at a downtown bar
That required police intervention,
Pupil Number Two and the university
Parted company for good.

The tutor's third pupil was entirely different,
A scholarship baseball player
Ineligible as a freshman to play for the varsity,
But so rapidly famed on campus that
Other students flocked to fall baseball practice
To watch him take his turn in the batting cage,
And thus saw him launching baseballs
To the far reaches of the practice field
And into the trees beyond its fences.
So talented an athlete was the young man that
After fall baseball practice ended,
He tried out for and made
The freshman basketball team.

It was toward the end of the basketball season
That the tutor first encountered him and
Found him as serious about
The history of Western Europe
As he had been about hitting baseballs.
Tutor and athlete met regularly
For the next two months,
With the athlete always prepared for the sessions,
The tutor relying on his "really good set of notes"
To guide the athlete through the assignments.

As the semester's end approached and
Final examinations loomed,
The athlete asked to borrow the tutor's notes
To help with his own review.
The tutor hesitated, reluctant to let
The precious collection out of his control,
But eventually agreed, realizing that
He would be unlikely ever to have
A need to consult those notes again.

The tutor handed over the notes and
As it turned out, never saw them again.
He did not see the athlete again
Before the semester ended, and
During the summer that followed,
The athlete's collegiate career
Came to an abrupt but profitable end
When a major league baseball team,
Recognizing the athlete's immense potential,
Signed him to a contract
Stunning for the time in its financial details.

The athlete eventually earned a degree,
But at a school half a continent away,
Closer to where he played,
Meanwhile hitting hundreds of home runs,
Driving in thousands of runs,
Building a career that would take him
To Cooperstown, New York, and enrollment in
Baseball's Hall of Fame.

The tutor sees the athlete occasionally now,
But only on television as the athlete,
Thicker of body, white of hair,
Comes trotting out of a dugout
In an untucked uniform shirt
During Hall of Famer introductions
At an All-Star Game,
Joining a platoon of old-timers
Along a first base line,
Still receiving a thunderous reception
From fans who had followed
His long and storied career.

When the tutor sees the athlete again,
He recalls those decades-ago cram sessions
In Yaz's sixth-floor dorm room.
Sometimes he wonders
What ever happened to
That really good set of notes on
The history of Western Europe.

Patriots

A Thursday evening in October.
A National League Divisional playoff game.
The hometown Nationals,
The World Champion Chicago Cubs.
The banks of arc lights atop the grandstands
Bright against the blue-black of the night sky,
The lights shining brightly down
On the broad emerald expanse of the outfield.
A splendid night for baseball.

Before the game, a familiar ritual,
The National Anthem.
As the music plays,
A spectator, a young woman in a broad-brimmed hat,
Kneels, acting in her own small way
In solidarity with dozens of professional athletes,
Football players, who kneel during the anthem
To call to the nation's attention
A current manifestation of
The nation's original sin.

Three young men sitting above her,
Already drunk, the first pitch not yet thrown,
Take offense at the woman's posture.
They leave their own seats,
Approach hers from the rear,
Berate her for her lack of patriotism,
For her disrespect for the nation's flag.
Standing behind the kneeling woman
With her broad-brimmed hat,
The patriots give physical expression

To the offense they have taken,
Pulling and poking at the hat brim.
The woman, still kneeling, turns,
Asks them to stop.
They ignore her and
Once her back is again turned,
They resume their pulling and poking.
No one nearby intervenes.
The harassment continues.

At length the young woman
Rises to her feet,
Walks to the nearest aisle,
Climbs to the concourse above,
Disappears from sight.
Clustered behind the woman's empty seat,
The three patriots exchange high-fives,
Congratulate each other on their victory
In the land of the free and
The home of the brave.

III. ON THE WATER

Delaware Beach

The summer sky overhead
Is clear and cerulean,
Its reflection a darker cobalt on
The ever-shifting ocean surface.
Near the beach
The water turns brownish-green
As the breaking waves
Rumble and crash, and
The spray rises yellow-white
Into the baking mid-afternoon air.

A predator arrives,
A Black-headed Gull,
Orange of beak and leg,
Pale gray of body,
Black of wingtip.
It streaks down the beach
A few feet above the water line,
Like a jet fighter on a strafing run,
Eyes so sharply focused as to suggest
An eerie avian intelligence lurking behind them.

A bold and opportunistic feeder,
Wikipedia calls this gull, one with
An ecumenical diet.
Insects and fish, seeds and worms,
Scraps and carrion –
They are all are at risk
As this hungry scavenger
Looks for targets of opportunity,
For a late lunch.

The gull is gone in seconds,
Disappears down the beach to the south,
Towards the Maryland shoreline,
But the image of those searching,
Near-human eyes?
That image hangs in the salt-smelling air
Above the rippled shoreline behind.

East Bay Morning

A couple's bayside getaway
On their anniversary weekend.
No long escape from their suburban home:
Instead, arrival at a nineteenth-century inn
At mid-afternoon on a Friday,
Departure less than forty-eight hours later.

Awake and dressed before seven
On the brightly sunlit Saturday morning,
A careful descent from their third-floor room
Down a narrow wooden staircase
To the deserted first-floor dining room.
Too early for the inn's breakfast buffet
But not too early for a cup of hot coffee
From the urn on a dining room counter,
And not too early to take the coffee outside,
Across the inn's broad bayside lawn
To two Adirondack chairs
Perched near the water's edge.

Once settled, they surrender themselves
To the sights, the sounds,
The very feel of the early late July morning:
The high-pitched chirping of the crickets
In the trees and bushes behind them
A single line of throbbing, pulsating sound,
Rising, falling, rising again;
The gas-fired murmur of motorboat engines
Already out on the water;
The cruciform silhouette of a low-flying plane
Against the pale blue, cerulean sky,

Its engine a metallic snarl in the air;
The ever-moving, ever-rippling water,
Striped in shades of dull green, darker and lighter,
Sunlight dancing silver and gold on the ripples;
The rustle of wavelets lapping against
The tumbled rocks of the seawall;
The rocks bleached white and gray in the sunlight,
Shading brown where washed by the wavelets;
A gaggle of geese settling onto the surface of a nearby cove,
Honking noisily into the morning air;
The shorefront breeze whistling through
The stately, centuries-old trees bordering the lawn,
Caressing the cheeks of the couple;
The couple themselves quiet, attentive, mindful,
Listening to the birdsong of multiple species.

An occasion for gratitude,
Not merely for bayside
Sights and sounds and sensations,
But for life itself
In all its varied splendors.

East Bay Afternoon

After the lunch in St. Michael's,
A reconnaissance mission
Southeast, away from the bay,
Away from St. Michael's –
"Historic St. Michael's,"
The visitors' guide says –
Then south, through the wood-fringed farmland
In Deep Neck and Ferry Neck
To the ferry slip at Bellevue Landing.

A gravelly lot affords
A place to leave the car.
The couple walks down to the landing
To watch the ferry load.
A single-decked craft, open to the sky.
A life-jacketed woman directs
Eight autos on board.
Five passengers walk on too.
A toot on the ferry's horn,
Mooring lines are cast off, and
The ferry, white froth bubbling in its wake,
Churns away from the landing
Across the blue-gray waters
At the mouth of the Tred Avon
To the dock at Oxford.

As thick gray clouds roll across the sky from the west,
The couple, their ferry-viewing done, retreats to their car.
They head northwest, back to St. Michael's and
Their inn at Wades Point beyond.
Halfway there, the rains come, so heavy that

It might have been monsoon season in Myanmar.
A post office, already closed for the day,
Provides a parking lot refuge
From the rainwater streaming out of the sky and
Sluicing along the narrow two-lane highway.

At length, the rain subsides to a light drizzle and
The couple resumes their journey back to the inn,
Returns to their third-floor room.
But the storm is not yet over.
From a window they look out over the bay
Where they see a giant, many-decked cruise ship,
Carnival, Royal Caribbean, whatever,
Making its stately way down the bay from Baltimore,
Bound for the Atlantic and the Caribbean beyond.
Seen from a distance, it moves ever so slowly,
So slowly that it cannot outrun
The broad gray wall of another stormband
That moves from west to east across the water,
Overtakes the vessel, envelops it, hides it from view.

The couple, landlubbers, have never seen this before.
They huddle in their room as the stormband reaches the inn,
Swallows it whole, lashes at their window.
They are grateful for the spectacle that nature has provided,
Grateful too that they are not aboard that cruise ship.

Maine Coast, Summer Morning

From Florida and Maryland,
From New York and Massachusetts,
The family gathers to celebrate
A couple's half-century of marriage.

It is quiet on the beach in the early morning,
The only sounds the occasional calls of seabirds and
The rhythmic plashing of wavelets breaking
Only a few feet onto the wet sand.
No great waves here, no Banzai Pipeline
In this quiet inlet off Casco Bay and
The great Atlantic beyond.
The sands glisten silver
As each wavelet recedes.

The sea mist coming off the ocean,
Reminiscent of San Francisco Bay,
Has disappeared, evaporated,
The sun already bright in the sky overhead,
The sky's color a pale blue,
Fading to misty yellow at the horizon,
The water's color depending on
Its distance from the shore,
Glassily blue close in,
Then gray-green, blue-green, and finally,
A hundred yards offshore,
Catching the sunlight, a gleaming silver.

Fifty yards out, the surfers in their black rubber wetsuits
Lie prone and still on their boards,
Like seabirds floating low on the surface of the sea,

The boards leaping into the air
Whenever a surfer tries to stand and
Losing balance splashes into the water.
Not an easy thing to do,
This scrambling to one's feet
Atop a slippery-wet surfboard
Bobbing on the ever-shifting surface of the sea.

On the beach, children search for sand dollars
Uncovered by receding wavelets,
While adult couples stroll nearby,
Coffee cups in hand.

Dogs scamper across the sands,
Dry for a time, suddenly wet
As they romp through the shallows,
Then out of the water and
Sprinting across the sand,
Chasing each other.

Maine's Piping Plovers,
Identified as an endangered species
By a sign posted on the beach,
Skitter through the shallows.

To the left, off towards the neighboring headland,
High-booted fishermen stand in the shallows,
On the cast for seabass.

The peace of it all, silence sought and found,
The clamor of the great world left behind
If only for a week.
Mission accomplished.

IV. ON EDUCATION

Dilemma Dramatized

It was no "Blackboard Jungle,"
This hundred-year-old, all male, Jesuit prep school
Whose seven hundred students
Wore coats and ties to school every day,
But there were moments.

A Friday morning in November,
A senior Latin class
In the school day's first period,
Book Four of *The Aeneid* the subject matter.

The instructor a Jesuit scholastic
In his first year of teaching.
His ascetical training was behind him,
Along with a college degree
And a graduate degree in philosophy.
Theology studies lay ahead
After three years in high school classrooms.
Beyond theology,
Ordination and the priesthood.

The morning's challenge:
To instill in his twenty-five still-drowsy students
Some sense of the Mantuan poet's purpose
In presenting the dilemma that faced
The poem's shipwrecked hero, Aeneas the True.
Should he remain in Carthage
As spouse of its lovesick queen,
The redoubtable Dido, or resume his journey
To found the city of Rome
At the direction of the gods

Whose images he had carried away from
Burning Troy, the kingdom a victim of
The hollow-horse ruse of the wily Ulysses?

The teacher dramatizes the choice,
Extolling Dido's virtues,
Describing Aeneas's brilliant future
In Carthage as her consort.
He poses a series of questions:
"Why would he do this?
Why sail off into an uncertain future?
Why leave this beautiful woman?"

Not all of the students are drowsy.
At the back of the classroom,
One of the class clowns –
Not mean-spirited, but
Ebullient in his mischief-making –
Cannot contain himself.
He cups his hand and shouts,
"Aeneas was a queer."

The class, now wide awake,
Erupts in laughter.
The teacher's face reddens,
His eyes narrow.
He races down an aisle
To the joker's desk,
Seizes him by the front of his shirt, and
Says through clenched teeth,
"One more word out of you, buster, and
You'll get flipped out of here on your ass."

A murmur of mock fear runs through the class.
Mercifully for the teacher,
The bell ending the class rings.
The teacher gathers up his books and flees.
It is the last the class will see of him.

On Monday morning, the teacher does not appear.
In his stead, the school's principal strides into the classroom.
He is a Jesuit priest in late middle age,
A man of vast experience
As teacher and administrator
Who will brook no adolescent nonsense.
The sexual orientation of Aeneas the True
Will never again arise.
Playtime has ended.

Bus Ride West

It begins in late afternoon
In early January,
In the center of the city,
At the Trailways terminal,
Closely observed by William Penn
From his perch atop City Hall.
The bus is long and boxy,
Its silvery sides racing-striped in crimson.
Once loaded, it rolls west,
Across the mud-brown Schuylkill,
Angles northwest beside the river
To the interchange near Valley Forge,
Where George Washington spent
A harsh, historic winter,
On then to the turnpike beyond.
The road snakes west,
Passes south of Harrisburg,
North of Breezewood
Where the truckers gather,
Sways round twisting curves,
Dives into mountain tunnels.
In places, it is a bumpy ride.
The turnpike has seen better days.

Toward the back of the bus on its left side,
In a window seat,
The aisle seat beside him empty,
A young man sits,
Returning to his university
For finals and the second semester to follow.
He is reading a book, twentieth-century American history –

The Republican Roosevelt's New Nationalism,
The Progressive Era and Woodrow Wilson's New Freedom,
World War I, the Roaring Twenties, the Great Depression.
Though history is his major,
This reading is for pleasure.
He loves the subject,
Wishes his high school
Had offered more history courses,
And so he reads beyond the textbooks
For the courses in his major.

The bus approaches Pittsburgh,
The turnpike bending to the right,
Heading from west to northwest.
The darkness creeps up behind,
Out of the east.
The midwinter sun falls swiftly,
Dips below the mountains ahead.
The bus plunges ahead, into the gathering darkness,
The sky turning from gray to blue-black.

The bus arrives in the three-rivered city
On the banks of the Allegheny,
The Monongahela, and the mighty Ohio,
Home to Steelers, Pirates, and Penguins.
The stop there is brief,
A matter of a few minutes.
Passengers debark, passengers board.
The bus soon rolls out of the terminal.

A return to the turnpike, the direction still northwest
Towards Cleveland on the lake,
The bus angling out of Pennsylvania
Into Ohio, passing west of Youngstown.

In the fully-fallen night,
In the circle of light
From the lamp beneath the baggage rack,
The young man reads on.

In his book, Franklin Roosevelt
Replaces Herbert Hoover.
The historian-author has written that
The old order is in crisis.
The New Deal is about to begin.

It is largely dark in the bus now.
A pool of light forward,
Around the driver's seat,
A long thin strip of light
On the floor along the aisle,
A guide to evacuation
Should it ever be necessary,
A few shafts of reading-lamp light
Streaming down from beneath
The baggage racks.

The young man decides he has read enough,
For the moment at least.
The Works Progess Administration and
The Tennessee Valley Authority will still be there
When he begins to read again.
He reaches up, turns off the overhead light,
Closes his book, sits back in his seat.
He closes his eyes and drops briefly off to sleep,
Lulled by the muffled roar of the bus's engine.

He wakes to find his mind
Drifting towards the future,

His personal future above all.
It is not so much his immediate future
That he wonders about.
He knows how that will go –
First the end-of-semester finals,
Then the second semester,
With another set of finals to follow,
And then home to Philadelphia
For a summer job to help
With senior year expenses.
No, he wonders what kind of life he will have
After college and beyond.
He supposes that he will work at something,
But he does not yet know at what.
He has no firm idea of
Who he is or will become,
Or even of what he wants to become.
Perhaps that knowledge,
Of who he is and will become,
Will never be fixed,
Never sure, never certain,
Always subject to revision and refinement,
Always provisional, tentative, contingent.
His musing making little progress,
He closes his eyes again.

Another departure from the turnpike, and
The bus heads north,
To the dreary, near-deserted,
Dimly-lit Cleveland terminal,
Steeped in late-night gloom.
Cleaners are at work there,
Mopping and buffing the floors.

A scattering of exhausted travelers
Stretches out full-length
On hard wooden benches,
Snatching a few moments of
Thin and ragged sleep
Before their connections arrive.

The bus sets out again,
Back to the turnpike
For the long westward plunge
Through the Ohio flatlands,
Skirting the south shore of the great lake,
Passing Sandusky,
Heading for Toledo.
The window beside the young man
Is cold to the touch,
Cold like the night outside.
He looks to his left, into the night.
The occasional star winks
In the vast expanse of the blue-black sky.
Scattered lights glow in
Lonely farmhouse windows and
Cast pale reflections
On patches of snow in the fields.
Pole-mounted sodium lamps
Bathe in pinkish-yellow light
The lightly-traveled rural roads
That the turnpike crosses over.

The young man shivers and
Pulls his jacket more tightly about his body.
He is half-awake, half-asleep, and
His mind begins to drift again.

Will there be love in his future, he wonders,
The love of a woman?
And if it does happen,
Who will that woman be?
Her name, what will it be?
What kind of person will she be?
What will she look like?
Has he met her already,
In the neighborhood where he has grown up?
Or will she be someone out there,
In his future, yet to be encountered?
He does not know, cannot know,
Not for a while at least.
The answers will come, some day,
But for now, all he has are questions,
With the answers, as important as any in his life,
To be found, if at all,
Years, even decades later.
The young man curls up in his seat,
Tries to sleep again, with some success.
He wakes in Toledo
In early morning darkness.
A smaller terminal than Cleveland's
But no less dreary.
The stop is brief, the bus soon on its way again,
Back to the turnpike, heading west,
Leaving Ohio, entering Indiana.

Another hour or two and
The young man's journey nears its end,
In northern Indiana.
Ahead of the bus, the sky begins to brighten.
Behind it, the sun peeps over the horizon.
As the bus slows to leave the turnpike,

The young man looks to his left.
His university's iconic dome
Gleams golden in the early morning sunlight.
Atop the dome, the statue of the woman
Gleams golden too, against
The cloudless cobalt blue of the sky.

University life awaits him
And he will see
Where that will take him.
The past is fixed, unchanging,
But the future is fluid, uncertain,
Its shape yet to be determined.
The young man is neither sad nor joyful,
Vaguely aware that a mystery lies ahead,
To be discovered and explored,
The mystery of himself.

Marchers

It is early March in Charm City, and
The organizers of its Saint Patrick's Day Parade
Call the priest-headmaster of
The local Jesuit prep school.
Would the school be willing to
Send a contingent of its students
To march down Charles Street
In the parade?

The headmaster hesitates,
Asks for time to consider the offer.
The school has seven hundred students, all male.
He cannot order them all to march.
How many would volunteer
If offered the opportunity?
He does not know, but he is sure that
A small turnout would embarrass the school.
He turns for advice to
Senior members of the lay faculty.
The athletic director, who also coaches basketball
And teaches math, has long experience
In the motivation of teenage boys.
He suggests an academic carrot.
If individual teachers are agreeable,
Every student in their classes who marches
Will receive a participation reward,
An upward bump of a full letter grade
At the end of the next marking period.

Relieved, the headmaster endorses the project,
As do half a dozen teachers, and soon

Two hundred boys, the majority
Less than stellar in the classroom and
Likely in need of the offered bonus,
Sign up to march in suit coats and ties
As if on a school day.

On the day of the parade,
A cool, sunny, mid-March Sunday,
The school's contingent –
Including a handful of teachers
To maintain order among the students –
Gathers in the parade's assembly area.
A teacher wonders aloud whether
The boys' marching would improve
If they had something to march to,
Something Irish perhaps.
After all, it is a Saint Patrick's Day parade.
The athletic director –
Now march director pro tem –
Agrees that Irish music would help.

The parade unit immediately behind the boys
Is a marching band from another local high school,
Entirely composed of African-American youngsters,
Resplendent in maroon uniforms with gold trim and
Wearing glittering golden shakos, the kind that
Napoleon's Imperial Guard might have worn.

The athletic director approaches the band's director,
African-American like his charges.
Do his musicians know any Irish music?
"Sure do," the band director says.
"We can do 'When Irish Eyes Are Smiling.'
How about that?"

"Perfect," the athletic director says.
"Could you play it as we march?"
"You bet," the band director says.

And so it is, as the Jesuit students
Step off four abreast in fifty-man columns,
That the band begins to play,
First the brass, then the drums.
"When I" – boom, boom –
"Rish eyes" – boom, boom –
"Are smiling" – boom, boom, boom –
And the marchers rise to the occasion by
Keeping pace with a near-military precision
That astonishes their teachers,
Coordinating their steps
To the band's energy-charged version
Of a sentimental Irish-American ballad.

Shortly after the band begins to play and
The marchers step out – C students pursuing
An elusive B, D students seeking
An even more precious C –
A teacher decides to lead a cheer.
"Gimme an L," he bellows.
The marchers give him an L.
"Gimme an O," he bellows.
The students respond again.
On the spelling-out goes,
Until the last name of
A sixteenth-century Basque mystic
Echoes down the street, and
Thousands of sidewalk-lining spectators
Cheer on the students for their spirit and

The musicians for their original rendition
Of that sentimental ballad.

That parade took place decades ago,
But each year, when Saint Patrick's Day arrives,
One of the teachers who marched
Beside his students on that cool March Sunday
Recalls those golden shakos
Reflecting off windows along the parade route,
Hears again a saint's spelled-out,
Shouted family name, and
Hears too that lively reshaping
Of a poignant ethnic lullaby.
 "When I" – boom, boom –
"Rish eyes" – boom, boom –
"Are smiling" – boom, boom, boom.

Raymond

1

A program of promise
For students with promise.
Six weeks of summer enrichment
For rising eighth graders
From Charm City schools,
Middle and elementary,
Public and parochial,
Forty-eight boys in all,
Forty-three black, five white,
Riding a bus each day
To a suburban prep school
Run by a religious order
With some reputation
For success in education,
The boys identified
By teachers and counselors
As likely to benefit
From a summer of opportunity.

An all-Jesuit faculty,
Two priests and four scholastics,
All seasoned veterans
Of high school classrooms,
With six trusted high school students
To serve as tutors.
The modest budget,
Three thousand dollars,
Covered by grants
From two local foundations.

The summer's message to the boys,
Implicit in every activity:
You can do it,
You would not be here
If you could not.

The program assembled
To promote steady academic progress:
The language classes plowing
Through graded reading kits;
The composition classes publishing
A literary magazine;
The math classes advancing
To ninth grade algebra.
And in the afternoon,
In acknowledgement that
These were, after all,
Twelve-year-old boys,
An hour in the prep school pool,
Where teacher-student distinctions dissolved,
And games of water polo
Became games of dodge ball,
Which in turn became
Mass dunking contests,
With the boys clambering
Up the backs of teachers and tutors,
And the resulting leaning towers of humanity
Collapsing in great eruptions of
Chlorinated water.

It is all very fine and
After some initial grumbling
Over summertime school work,
The daily afternoon swims

Softening the blow,
Forty-seven boys out of forty-eight
Take to the program,
All but one,
All except Raymond,
Who does not want to be there.
His seventh grade teacher
Thought it would be good for him,
Spoke to his mother,
Who told Raymond he was going,
And so he went,
But his expression is a perpetual scowl, and
His body language a near
Horizontal slouch at his desk.
They make it clear:
Raymond does not want to be there,
Wants no part of this summer of promise.

2

The program is designed to inspire
As well as to educate.
The boys watch three films
Depicting the struggles of
People of color against the stacked deck of
Mid-century American life,
With "Raisin in the Sun" the finale.
Guest speakers arrive
To give voice to inspiration:
Three accomplished men of color –
A sociology professor from Morgan State,
A Maryland state legislator,
Baltimore's first black police captain –

And for aspiring major leaguers,
A rookie, right-handed Orioles pitcher
Who treasures his degree from Iowa State.

For reading material outside class,
The boys work their way
 Through biographies of minorities
Who overcame
The obstacles in their lives.

There are field trips:
The boys visit local colleges –
Morgan State, home of the Bears,
Loyola, home of the Greyhounds –
Wander across tree-shaded,
Grass-lined campus walks,
Visit art exhibitions and
Marvel at chemical reactions in
University laboratories.

It is a fine program,
But Raymond is not impressed.
Still he scowls, still he slouches.
He does not want to be there.

3

What Raymond does not know is
That every afternoon,
After the bus from the high school
Has taken the boys downtown,
The teachers and the tutors gather,
Review every single boy in the program,

On the lookout for boys
Who need special attention
In class or outside.

It is inevitable:
Raymond's name comes up.
The priest-director poses the question:
"What about Raymond?
The scowl, the slouching,
Everything about him says that
He doesn't want to be here."
The scholastics and the tutors
Offer their opinions.
"He seems kind of sullen," says one.
Finally, the other priest,
Professionally a math teacher,
Presents his amateur psychological assessment:
"I don't think he's really sullen.
The sullenness is a mask
He hides behind.
He's just afraid,
Afraid of being treated badly,
By us, by the tutors, by the other boys.
He looks at us,
Our little all-white faculty and tutors,
And he's afraid that we won't treat him fairly
Because he's black,
Even though forty-two other kids
Look pretty much like him.
And he's waiting for
The other kids to mock him.
Kids can be cruel.
I'm sure he knows that.
And he's also afraid because

We are all strangers to him.
Not just us, but the other students,
Black and white,
They are strangers to him too.
He's the only kid from his school here.
He doesn't know anyone.
He's alone.
He's shielding himself in advance
From the pain or shame
Or humiliation he would feel
If he let his guard down,
Made himself vulnerable and then
He was treated badly –
By the faculty, the tutors, the other boys.
We have to show him
That we will not treat him badly.
We've got to make him feel that
He's not alone, that he's one of us.
That means respect, patience,
Kindness, encouragement, whatever.
Once he learns to trust us,
Well, then, he'll be a different boy."

Discussion follows, a consensus forms.
The diagnosis is accepted, and
A conspiracy hatched.
The priests are part of it,
The scholastics and tutors too.
Raymond will be immersed in kindness,
Smothered with respect and encouragement.
His sullenness will be ignored,
Met with good humor and
Endless patience.
The teachers and tutors will put on an act,

Making a special effort but hiding it,
Attending specially to Raymond
Without appearing to do so,
Pretending that he is just a boy
Like the other forty-seven in the program.
Kindness, respect, patience, encouragement,
A steady diet of them for Raymond and
The conspirators will see what happens.

4

It does not happen all at once,
But slowly the treatment begins to work
As the conspirators had hoped it would.
The steady drip of kindness,
Patience, encouragement, good humor,
Takes effect.
A little each day,
The façade of sullenness erodes,
Begins to crumble.
And it is a façade,
Underneath it a frightened little boy
Who wants desperately to be respected,
To be liked, even loved.

Raymond is less hostile,
Less distant.
He scowls less often,
He even sits up straighter at his desk.
In class he raises his hand,
Asks questions, volunteers answers,
Risks mockery from his classmates.
But it does not come.

There is jeering to be sure,
But it is good-natured,
The same every other boy gets.

He is not good at games,
But the pool is different.
He joins in the after-lunch rough-housing there
Where water polo becomes dodge ball and
Dodge ball becomes mock attempts at drowning.
It does not take much skill
To climb on the backs
Of the teachers and tutors
And try to drag them under.
When Raymond succeeds – he often needs help –
He is surprised that they compliment him,
Even as they vow vengeance,
And he does not mind that
Because it is all part of the game,
An entirely new experience for him.

One of the tutors, big for his age,
Presents an especially inviting target
For hurled dodge balls and dunking attacks,
But he ignores the balls
That bounce off his back and shoulders and
As for the attempted dunkings,
He shakes them off easily,
Just as he will shed would-be tacklers
A few years later
When he will play tight end for Notre Dame and
A few years after that, for the Chicago Bears, and
Raymond can watch him on television
And boast of dunking him in a high school pool.

5

The summer program draws rapidly to a close:
The boys competing in math class
To get to the blackboard,
The rising eighth graders eager to show
Their mastery of that ninth grade algebra text;
The faculty collecting the boys' essays and
Publishing them in the literary magazine, and
The boys beaming when
They find their essay titles and
Their names in the table of contents.

On graduation night in the high school auditorium,
Before proud parents, relatives, friends,
The boys present two scenes from *Julius Caesar,*
Reenacting a conspiracy formed two millennia before –
The mob exuberantly shouting "Hail, Caesar";
Caesar himself shoving the soothsayer
Around the stage for daring to suggest
That he "beware the Ides of March";
Brutus and his fellows happily splashing ketchup on
The white sheet that serves as Caesar's toga;
Raymond, he formerly of the scowl and slouch,
An enthusiastic assassin.

After the dramatics,
An award ceremony and,
In a final touch devised
By latter-day conspirators
Focused on Raymond rather than Caesar,
An award for Raymond,
Something about perseverance, dedication, effort.
A consensus had previously developed –

Raymond had to win something.
The summer could not end
Until he had won something.
The transformation could not go unacknowledged.

He is stunned when he hears his name.
The applause rises around him
As he walks unsteadily to the stage
To receive his medal.
He ducks his head in embarrassment.
But it is embarrassment by joy, and
Even though he tries to suppress
The smile that spreads across his half-hidden face,
He fails.

The applause accompanies him back to his seat.
It comes from the faculty, the tutors,
The other boys, all of them, the guests too.
He has never won anything before,
No one has ever applauded him before,
And if there are tears in his eyes
When he takes his seat,
There is a reason.

Raymond has indeed proven
That he could do it.

Interest Revived

He was twenty-one,
About to enter a religious order
Where a vow of poverty would be taken,
Yet in response to an obscure prompting
That at some point in his life
He would become involved with poetry,
He went to a bookstore and
Bought a collection of letters
Written by an insurance executive
Famous for his poetry.
The purchase puzzled even the buyer.
He knew that the letters
Would have to be left behind
When he entered the order.

He knew something of the poet-executive,
A passing acquaintance developed
In a class on modern verse where
In a collection compiled by the dean
Of poetry anthologizers,
He had encountered a man with a blue guitar,
Had gotten an idea of order at Key West,
Had envisioned the complexities of
Women in dressing gowns on Sunday mornings,
But that was all.

Why had he bought that collection of letters?
Did he have some vague intimation that
He was not suited for religious life,
Would return at some point in the future
To the world he had left behind and

Would have time and leisure
To savor the letters of the poet-executive
As he turned his life in another direction?
But then it was time to go,
To enter the order on one of
The great feasts of the Virgin Mary,
The letters of the poet-executive remaining behind,
To languish unread for many years and
Ultimately to disappear during
A rearrangement of the family home.

As it turned out, more than a decade later,
He discerned that he was not
Ultimately suited to the religious life,
And at length that obscure prompting returned,
Not fully understood or appreciated,
But leading over the succeeding years
To the slow, steady accumulation of volumes of poetry,
Metaphysicals like Donne and Marvell and Herbert,
Symbolists like Baudelaire and Rimbaud and Mallarmé,
American classics like Dickinson and Whitman,
Englishmen like Hopkins and expatriates like Eliot.
Paperbacks in the main, new and used,
Piling up in bookcases,
Waiting to be opened and read,
Behind the accumulation a vague feeling lurking
That he would someday get round
To reading them and they would
Serve, in the fullness of time, as
Inspiration for an engagement with poetry,
Even an attempt to write poetry himself.

Not until several decades after that first bookstore purchase
Would he return to the poet-executive and his poetry and,

In a long-delayed seed-sprouting,
Begin himself to write poetry, and
In a completion of the circle of his interest,
Acquire a biography of the poet-executive
To learn more about the man
Whose letters he had not read
So many years before.

Aspiration

The Beloved Disciple wrote it first:
"The Word became flesh, and
Dwelt among us,
Full of grace and truth."
John wrote in Aegean-washed,
Ionian-shored Ephesus,
Or so the scripture scholars tell us,
And composed the Prologue,
Passage of extraordinary depth,
Identifying the Word
As God's universal agent
Of creation and providence,
Reflecting not only the theological insights
Of the Old Testament –
Wisdom at God's side, a master craftsman,
Ever at play in God's presence,
At play everywhere in God's world,
Delighting in the company of the sons of men –
But of other sources too,
The Jewish rabbinic tradition,
The Christian tradition of the Apostolic Age,
Of Hellenicism and Stoicism as well.
Remarkable achievement
For a Galilean fisherman,
A son of Zebedee,
Writing of a carpenter's son from Nazareth.

The poet's task is far humbler:
To take the flesh, the raw material
Offered by the poet's own experiences in the flesh –
The seeing and hearing and tasting,

The smelling and touching – and
Transform that fleshly material
Into words of grace and truth.
A matter of aspiration,
Rather than assured achievement,
But a worthy task anyway,
The poet making a much diminished
But still new creation,
As the Word had made the first creation,
As the Word in becoming flesh had made
A second, more significant creation.

The Word the instrument of God's communication,
The poet's words the instruments
Of human communication.
The Word bringing light to the darkness of the world,
A darkness moral and spiritual as well as natural,
The poet aspiring, struggling, to bring a lesser light
To the world by transforming flesh into language and
Communicating, always imperfectly, the glory and wonder
Of human experience in the flesh.

The Word by becoming flesh and entering history
Giving meaning to history,
The poet already in the midst of history,
Seeking to give meaning to the experience
Of the flesh in history,
His medium mere words.

V. NO END TO CONFLICT

A Soldier of the Great War

He was only sixteen,
But big for his age, and
When he walked into the recruiting office
As the nation was building an army
To fight the war to end all wars,
No questions were asked.
The Twenty-Eighth Division,
Pennsylvania National Guard,
With its bloody bucket of a shoulder patch,
Was glad to have him, and
So off to war he went.

He came home a year and a half later,
A hero of sorts, with two medals,
One with a rainbow ribbon and
A metal bar the color of pewter
That read "Meuse-Argonne Campaign,"
The other a Purple Heart,
George Washington in silhouette,
Courtesy of the Kaiser's army
From a chance encounter in a French forest.

He came home with a taste for alcohol too,
Not so heroic a thing.
No Germans to fight then,
Just the bottle.
The battle lasted three decades and more.
There was one woman
Who might have saved him,
But the romance did not last.
Alcohol cost him the woman,
Just as it cost him jobs.

Eventually he could find work
Only as a watchman, four to midnight,
After the factories had closed for the day.

He still lived at home,
With his parents,
Well into his thirties.
Every day he rose late,
Said he was going out
For a beer before work.
Every day his mother
Packed a lunch for him,
Sat with it in her lap
At the front window
Overlooking the street outside,
Waiting for him to come home and pick it up,
But often he did not, and
Another job search would follow.

He had liked the outdoor life in the army, and
During the Depression, he found a temporary haven
In the Civilian Conservation Corps
As he cut trails through national forests,
Planted hundreds of trees,
Helped to pave long stretches of road.

Afterwards, when war in Europe loomed again,
He found another refuge in
The army that had once been his home.
He enlisted again, but was soon discharged.
He was close to forty and
The army wanted younger men,
Of whom millions were available.
All he brought home with him
From that second enlistment

Were tales of meeting rattlers and copperheads
During maneuvers in the Alabama woods,
Tales that mesmerized his city boy nephews.

There were high moments
In his lonely, bachelor life,
As when he took a nine-year-old nephew
To a night game at the A's old Shibe Park
To watch Bob Feller pitch for the Indians,
And both strained their eyes in the dusk
To follow the path of Rapid Robert's fastball.

But those moments were not frequent.
When his parents died,
He moved in with his sister and her husband,
And there were evenings,
After he had been out on the town,
When he staggered home and
His brother-in-law had to put him to bed
As his nephews watched wide-eyed.
With a heavy drinking brother of his own,
The brother-in-law had performed the chore before.

The thirty-odd years since the war had taken their toll,
And so it was sad, but no great surprise when
On a steamy overcast Sunday afternoon in July
The call came from the factory
Where he stood watch at night and on weekends
That someone had found him,
Dead of a heart attack,
Slumped in his cramped watchman's hut
On the edge of an empty parking lot,
Alone at the end and,
In his way, another victim of the Great War.

Historic Preservation

Italy in the late summer of 1944.
The Allies have taken Rome.
The Germans have retreated northwards,
Beyond the Arno, even as
Other Allied armies are sweeping across France,
East from Normandy, north from the Riviera.
The names of towns and rivers
That have echoed around the world
For most of the past year,
Salerno and Cassino and Anzio,
The Rapido and the Volturno,
Fade slowly from memory.
Italy has become a backwater in the war,
But even in a backwater,
The war goes on.

On an August morning, two young men
Climb a flight of rickety wooden stairs
To the belfry of a church tower
On the south bank of the Arno,
Across from the city of Pisa.
The two men are second lieutenants
In the American army, forward observers
For a chemical mortar battalion,
Their mission to scan
The Arno's German-occupied far bank
And the environs of Pisa beyond
For targets of opportunity,
And if such targets presented themselves,
To call a mortar barrage,
High explosive and white phosphorus,
Down upon them.

In a few days, American artillery will lay down a barrage
And the infantry will climb into small boats
And paddle across the Arno, and
the German machineguns will open up,
And the war will begin in earnest again.

But for now, the front is quiet,
And the two young men,
Thinking it will do no harm
To enjoy an occasional sip of wine
While they wait, perhaps in vain,
For a target to appear across the river,
Have equipped themselves
Not only with a two-way radio
To communicate with battalion headquarters,
But with a jug of rough red wine apiece.

The hot, sunny August day passes slowly and
To ease the boredom that arises
From staring fruitlessly across the Arno
At the river's deserted far bank,
The two lieutenants allow themselves
From time to time a drink or two
From their jugs of wine.

Finally, in the late afternoon,
A dozen German soldiers,
Seeking relief from the heat,
Emerge from a patch of woods
Near the Arno's far bank,
Strip off their field-gray uniforms, and
Plunge into the river for a swim.

Here at last is a target for the two lieutenants.
Roused from an alcohol-induced torpor,

They giddily call in the day's first fire mission,
Radioing the map coordinates
For the bathers' location
Back to the battalion's mortar batteries.

The mortarmen, perhaps grateful for something to do
On a sweltering August day, respond promptly.
Soon the lieutenants hear shells passing overhead and
Watch them fall into the midst of
The splashing German swimmers.
The sight of deadly water spouts
Erupting in the river around them
Is more than enough for the Germans,
Who scramble out of the river,
Snatch up their clothing, and
Sprint into the woods on the far bank.

In the quiet that follows,
The lieutenants congratulate themselves
On the disruption of the German swimming party,
Rewarding themselves with further sips from
The now near-empty wine jugs.
That was fun, they tell each other, and
Wonder whether they can find another target.
They look across the river again and
In the distance spy, not for the first time,
A large church with an adjoining cylindrical tower
That tilts dramatically to one side.
Reasoning that the tower appears
Ready to collapse soon of its own accord,
They decide to help it along.
They plot the tower's coordinates,
Radio them back to battalion, and
Sit back, waiting for the barrage to begin.

Long moments pass in silence.
The lieutenants are puzzled.
Why aren't the mortars firing?
Then heavy footsteps sound
On the bell tower's creaking stairs.
Four burly military policemen
Burst into the belfry,
Confiscate the wine jugs,
Place the lieutenants under arrest.

Back at battalion headquarters,
Another officer, another second lieutenant,
Had plotted the coordinates
Supplied by the two observers.
Shaking his head in disbelief,
He picked up a field telephone,
Cancelled the fire mission,
Summoned the military police.

In the late summer of 1944,
Much of Italy, from Messina in the south
To Florence in the north,
Lay in ruins, but in Pisa a tilted tower
Survived to lean another day.

Isaac's Story

His name was Isaac,
And he was a Jew,
And like so many other Jews
Caught up in the maelstrom
That was Europe in the Second World War,
He found himself in a concentration camp,
Safe for the moment
From the gas chambers and
The mass shootings,
But with death drawing nearer each day
From hunger and illness and overwork
And other assorted cruelties,
Even as the war's end approached.

Then, one late spring morning
In the seventh year of the war,
Isaac and his fellow prisoners
In their broad-striped prison costumes
Woke to find their guards gone,
In flight from the Russians no doubt,
The vengeance coming from the Eastern Front
Enough to inspire all-consuming fear.
The prisoners, ever on starvation's edge,
Thought first of food and set out
For the camp commandant's home,
Hoping to find food there.

As they rooted in the commandant's garden,
A truck filled with soldiers
Rolled through the camp's gate.
The prisoners shrank back,

Thinking the guards had returned,
But no, the uniforms were different,
Brown rather than field-gray.
These soldiers were Americans,
And the prisoners gathered to stare at them
With wonder and relief.
A single jeep carrying three men
Followed the truck into the camp.
The driver was a sergeant,
Who braked the jeep to a stop, got out, and
Walked over to the huddled, emaciated prisoners.
Isaac stood near the front of the group and
For some reason unknown to Isaac,
The sergeant focused on him.

The sergeant took a canteen from his web belt,
Unscrewed the cap that doubled as a cup,
Poured the cup full of water, and
Extended it to Isaac.
But Isaac did not accept the extended cup
For the sergeant was a black man,
And from childhood Isaac had been taught,
And had embraced the teaching,
That blacks were inferior,
Less than fully human, unclean,
A race to be avoided, even despised.
Accepting anything from one of them,
Even a drink of water, unthinkable.
And so Isaac stared at the sergeant's
Extended, coffee-colored, cup-holding hand,
But did not move to take the cup.

The sergeant was patient,
Perhaps sensing what was in Isaac's mind,

Perhaps having known whites to shrink
From contact with him in his own country.
It did not matter, for he was patient, and
He kept his cup-holding hand extended,
Waiting on Isaac.
And as the sergeant waited,
It at length occurred to Isaac
That he was no less racist
Than the gray-uniformed men
Who had guarded him in the camp,
And it was only then,
As Isaac felt himself filling with shame,
That he stretched out his own trembling hand and
Took the cup from the sergeant's hand.

Decades later, on another continent,
At an interfaith conference,
A priest gave a talk.
When his talk was over,
An elderly man approached and
Said he needed to talk with him.
He told the priest a story,
A story about a black sergeant
With an extended, cup-holding hand.
When the elderly man had finished,
The priest asked him why he chose
The priest to tell the story to.
The man said he had done so
Because he knew the priest
Would tell the story to many others.

Isaac was right.

Wars of Religion

The Christians and the Muslims
Had clashed before on the Mediterranean.
More than four hundred years before,
Don Juan of Austria, bastard son of an emperor,
Half-brother of a king,
Had led two hundred Holy League galleys
Into Greece's Gulf of Patras and
With his larger, better-armed vessels
Crushed the more numerous galleys of
Ali Pasha's Ottoman fleet in
The Battle of Lepanto,
Securing the western half of the great sea
For centuries to come.

In these more modern times,
Christians and Muslims have met yet again
On the broad waters of the Mediterranean,
This time on a smaller scale,
Not in galleys and galleasses
With lateen sails and banks of rowers,
But in a single, fragile, overcrowded rubber dinghy.
They were all of them migrants,
The Christians not from Barcelona or Genoa
Or Venice like the warriors of the Holy League,
But from Nigeria and Ghana,
The Muslims not from Istanbul
Or Tunis or Alexandria like Ali Pasha's Ottomans,
But from Ivory Coast, Senegal, and Mali.

In battered pickup trucks,
They came separately, these Christians and Muslims,

Across Algeria's vast wastes and
The scorched Sahara sands,
Their overland journeys ending on the Libyan shore –
Their arrival there a miracle in itself –
Where with little more than the clothes on their backs
They boarded, Christians and Muslims alike,
The sole craft available and
Set out across the Mediterranean
For the promised lands of Sicily, Italy, and
The rest of Europe beyond.

There were a hundred and five of them,
These migrants, Christian and Muslim,
And some Muslim men among them,
Fifteen of them, judging the number too high,
Feared that the dinghy would capsize,
Spill its passengers into the sea.
They argued with some of the Christian men,
Strangers by religion and nationality,
About the boat's seaworthiness.
At length, the Muslims turned on the Christians,
First with threats, then with action,
Seizing a dozen Christian men
And throwing them overboard.
The dinghy, lighter, less crowded, went on its way,
The Christian men left behind to drown,
Their hopes for deliverance
From war and fear and famine
To be swallowed up by the sea.

An Italian naval vessel happened upon the dinghy,
Took it in tow, brought it to safety at Palermo.
Authorities interviewed the ninety-odd survivors,
Learned of the threats, the attack on the Christian men,

Their abandonment in the Mediterranean.
They arrested the Muslims responsible,
Charged them with multiple homicides,
Aggravated by religious hatred.

As a certain Southern novelist once wrote,
The occasion a metaphorical requiem for a nun,
"The past is never dead.
It's not even past."

Pilgrimage

For the couple, a trip to the Basque country
To attend the wedding of a daughter's friend,
But a week in the City of Light first,
The Left Bank, Notre Dame,
The Musée D'Orsay, the Arc de Triomphe,
Montmartre, Sacre Coeur, and the Eiffel Tower,
And in the middle of the week, a side trip by train
To the northwest, towards the Channel,
The ride from the Gare St. Lazare
Quiet, smooth, fast,
Past the towering basilica at Lisieux,
The town home to a Little Flower,
And beyond to Normandy and its beaches,
The beaches forever famous,
But not for bathing.

A change of trains at Caen,
Risen from its 1944 ruins, and
On to Bayeux, the last stop on the train.
On the couple's way to a rendezvous
With their guide at the Place de Quebec,
They happen upon and circle around
The renowned tapestry that offers
A view of an earlier invasion.
Lunch follows at a bistro, Coady Fortier,
That appeals to select tourists
With a sign announcing "English Spoken Here."

Afterwards, a short walk to the Place de Quebec,
A brief wait on a bench in the sunlit square, and
The arrival of their seven-passenger van with

Five people already seated within.
The driver-guide – her name is Sabrina –
Welcomes the couple, seats them, and
Drives northwest, out of Bayeux,
Towards the first stop on the tour,
The promontory called Pointe du Hoc.
En route, she provides a brief account of
The causes and events of the Second World War
In western Europe – the 1940 German offensive,
Dunkirk, the fall of France, the Occupation –
That led up to June 1944 and the Allied invasion.

At Pointe du Hoc, where on D-Day
American Rangers climbed sheer cliffs
To assault an artillery battery
That menaced the invasion beaches
Only to find that the Germans
Had moved the guns inland,
The van's passengers descend
Into a concrete bunker and look out on
The English Channel through gunports that offer
The view the German defenders had on D-Day.

From Pointe du Hoc, Sabrina drives east to the beaches,
Passing along the way another relic of the war,
An 88-millimeter dual-purpose artillery piece,
The legendary "88" so dreaded by Allied soldiers.

At Omaha Beach, Sabrina parks the van
Near the American National Guard Memorial
Overlooking the beach,
Beneath the bluffs where the Germans
Had placed their machine-gun nests.
The memorial is well-placed.

The Twenty-Ninth Division, Virginia National Guard,
The Blue and Gray Division, had landed there,
Its men dying by the dozens.

The van's passengers get out, stretch, and
Cross the beachfront road to the memorial,
Where they stand and look out
Across the broad sunlit beach,
The sand darker in places, wet
Where the tide has just receded,
The hundreds of yards of open beach
Reaching out towards the Channel waters,
Empty on this early September day,
But filled with ships on a June morning
Almost seventy years before.

Tacticians say that of all military operations,
An amphibious landing on a hostile shore
Is the most hazardous. The Royal Dublin Fusiliers
Who assaulted Cape Helles at Gallipoli
In April of 1915 would not disagree.
Neither would the men of the Second Marine Division
Who waded across the lagoon at Tarawa
Six months before D-Day.
Omaha Beach was no exception to the rule.

Children fly kites on the beach and
Dogs chase balls thrown by their masters.
As the couple stand watching and
Grasp how broad the beach is,
The man recalls iconic images,
Preserved in grainy, black-and-white newsreels
From that gray, overcast Tuesday morning in 1944,
Images of men, bulky figures

Burdened with sixty pounds of equipment,
Stumbling out of landing craft,
Wading slowly through the surf,
Trudging onto the sand,
Bent over as if advancing
Against a gale-force wind,
Past mine-strewn wooden stakes and
Steel hedgehogs designed
To disembowel landing craft,
Some of those men crumpling
In black heaps on the wet sand,
Never to rise again,
As the bullets from caves
In the bluffs sought them out.

The man recalls other filmed images too,
Wonders what it must have been like
For the men in the landing craft
Approaching that beach,
What they must have felt
As German bullets hammered
Against the ramps of the landing craft,
And the men knew that
When the ramps dropped and
They stumbled into the surf
In the face of that hail of bullets,
They would be as close to death
As they had ever been in their lives.

It is time for the tour to continue.
Sabrina bundles her charges into the van and
Drives east again, along the coastal road
To the American cemetery at Colleville-sur-Mer,
Where so many of the men

Who had crumpled to the sand in death
On Bloody Omaha are buried.
The cemetery is carefully tended,
The long parallel rows of white crosses
Stretching away in the distance,
Small groups wandering among the crosses,
Searching for a familiar name.

Upon the request of the woman in the couple,
Sabrina leads the van's passengers
To the Garden of the Missing
Beyond the cemetery's memorial
Where on one of the limestone panels enclosing the garden
The woman finds what she is looking for,
The name of a cousin carved into the stone.
Having lied about his age in order to enlist,
He had been still a teenager, her cousin,
When in the weeks after D-Day,
His ship was torpedoed and
He was lost at sea in the English Channel.

On to Arromanches then,
Where the British had landed,
Where remains of the invasion's artificial harbors –
"Mulberries," they were called –
Crouch like beached whales
In the shallow water offshore.
The gift shop on the beachfront
Throngs with customers in search of souvenirs.
On Sabrina's recommendation,
The couple buys a box of caramels,
Soon to be consumed, the guide vouching
For their quality from long experience.
They purchase no other souvenirs,

No toy soldiers or plastic models of tanks or howitzers,
No picture books or unit patches.
Their memories of the broad beach that was Omaha,
That men once trudged across to their deaths,
Of the long rows of white crosses at Colleville-sur-Mer,
Of a teenaged Vermonter's name cut into a panel
On the wall that borders on the Garden of the Missing –
They would be enough.

VI. ALL IN THE FAMILY

On the Bridge

The father's workday ended at four-thirty, and
Though he worked north of Camden in Jersey,
His ride routinely got him to his home
Across the Delaware in South Philly by five-fifteen,
Thanks to a river-spanning, dead-poet-honoring bridge.

A surprise then one summer afternoon
When five-fifteen came and went
Without the father's appearance.
In those pre-cellphone days,
His wife and five children were left
To wonder where he was.
Six o'clock came and went,
Six-thirty too, and still no father.

Finally, close to seven,
He called. From a pay phone,
Outside a hospital emergency room.
There had been an accident,
A collision, on the bridge.
He had been riding unsecured –
No seatbelts in those mid-fifties days –
In the front passenger seat.
The collision had thrown him forward, and
He had struck his head on the windshield,
Cracked and spider-webbed from the crash,
But was otherwise all right,
Was getting a ride, would soon be home.

Palpable relief in the household,
Great anxiety as well.

How hard had his head
Hit that windshield?

Half an hour later, a car pulled up
In front of the rowhouse home.
The father emerged slowly,
Walked unsteadily toward the house,
A blood-stained bandage encircling his head
At forehead level, and a second bandage,
Bloodstained too, covering his nose.
He climbed the four steps leading
To the front door and fell through
The now-open door into his wife's arms.
The children, the five of them,
Clustered around, hugging their parents
In whatever way they could,
The father saying sheepishly that
His nose had been cut open –
He would wear the scar
Until the end of his life –
And was probably broken too.
His wife said it did not matter
As long as he was home and safe.

The relief in that seven-person embrace
Was not unalloyed, but rather undermined
By a sense of how vulnerable they all were,
A sense of what might have been –
The husband and father gone in an instant,
The collision shattering forever
The stability of the family's daily routine.
It would never be quite the same again.

Refrigerator Door

It is evening as the father
Enters the darkened kitchen.
He turns on the light, and
For the thousandth time or so,
He scans the dozens of photos
Magnet-clipped to the refrigerator door.

It is summer in one.
The girl and the boy,
Perhaps three and five,
Perch on the steps that lead
Up to the backyard terrace,
The girl in a pink-and-white
Seersucker playsuit,
The boy in a red, white, and blue
Superhero T-shirt.
Both are innocent, earnest, open-eyed,
Unafraid, squinting a little in bright sunlight,
Smiling ever so slightly.

They are older in other door-clipped images,
From the high school years, the college years.
Both athletes, good ones,
The girl a midfielder in field hockey,
Soccer and lacrosse,
The boy a tailback in football,
A goalie in lacrosse,
Both collecting awards and
Championships along the way.
And then the graduations –
The caps, the gowns,

The diplomas lifted in triumph –
Two from college,
Two more from law school.

The refrigerator images end then,
As the girl and the boy,
Now young woman and young man,
Advance into adulthood.

The moments captured in those photos
Fade into the past,
Each day less easily retrieved:
Times beyond price,
Not fully treasured when
So fleetingly present,
An occasion now, small but real,
For a parent's regret.

Holiday Stumble

It starts with pre-Christmas purchases,
Multiple bottles of Pinot Noir,
Sauvignon Blanc, and Chardonnay.
Next comes the buyer's brain-dead decision:
To lug the bottle-filled cardboard box
Down a flight of carpeted steps,
From the first floor to the basement,
In bulky winter clothing and
Rubber-soled boat shoes.

Not a long flight of steps,
Only nine of them,
But long enough.

Three steps from the bottom
A boat shoe catches on a carpeted step.
The box, unhelpfully unwieldy,
Pulls its carrier off-balance.
It falls first, to the carpeted floor,
The carrier following,
Tumbling in a heap beside it,
His knee bent at an angle
It was not designed for.

Cushioned by the sides of the box and
The carpeted floor, the wine bottles do not shatter.
The carrier is less fortunate.
His knee badly wrenched,
He will soon visit an orthopedist
For a shot of cortisone.

Before then, though,
Even as he begins to tell
The sad tale of his stumble and
The cause of his limp,
Relatives and friends will ask
But a single burning question:
What happened to the wine?

Eighty Arriving

He watches his eightieth birthday come and go
With a kind of wonder.
At thirty, he thought his life was over.
In many ways, it had just begun.

He is a survivor of sorts.
His father died at fifty-nine,
His mother at seventy-four,
One younger brother at sixty-nine,
Another at fifty-three,
A younger brother-in-law at forty-two,
A younger sister-in-law at fifty-four,
And yet here he is,
In his ninth decade, still counting.

Yes, with creaking knees and
Carrying ten extra pounds, and
Yes, with coronary artery disease,
But thanks to two stents and
Five pills a day, under control.

Twelve years retired,
With time to look back,
Take stock of his life,
Reflect on the fragmented mysteries of memory,
Why some memories stand out
But not thousands of others,
Fifty-year-old shards of memory preserved,
Events of last week lost forever.

In the stock-taking, moments of pain and humiliation,
Shame and embarrassment, moments of regret

Over deeds left undone, words left unsaid,
Situations handled badly or not at all.
Regret for so many stupidities of commission,
So many failures by omission,
Regret for not saying "thank you" often enough,
To parents, siblings, other relatives,
To friends, teachers, even strangers,
To all who helped him
To get where he is today,
Entering decade number nine.

Yes, in that fragment-filled memory bank,
Moments of success as well,
Of small-scale triumphs even,
But he does not dwell on them,
Knowing the self-indulgence of such dwelling,
Those moments only part of his story.

How swift the passage of the years.
He would have paid more attention,
Shown more appreciation if he had realized
They would disappear so quickly.

Little he can do now
About the moments he regrets.
Nothing, really, except
Learn from those moments,
Try to avoid their like in the future so that
In the years left to him
The burden of regret will be
Just a bit lighter.

And all is not lost, swamped in a sea of regret.
As he reflects, he appreciates once again

That he found the love of his life at eighteen,
But did not fully realize it until
He had gone one way and she another,
Only to find her again at thirty-eight,
Marry her a month short of forty,
Having found her for keeps this time,
That second finding greatly gifting his life,
Not with the marriage alone,
But with two children now adults as well, and
Yet another more recent gift, a first grandchild,
A seven-month-old girl named Claire.

No, his life had not ended at thirty.
A succession of new lives beginning
Lay ahead, decades in the future.

Afterlife

I'm hoping for an afterlife,
So I can see my parents once again, and
Apologize for not thanking them enough
When they were alive
For all they had done
For my sister, my brothers, and me,
Apologize for not telling them
Often enough how much I loved them.

No need for gilt-edged clouds
In my hoped-for afterlife,
Or for Gregorian chant from angel choirs.
No, just a place looking like
A rowhouse neighborhood in South Philly,
The kind of place where they poured out
So much love on the five of us,
A good place to see my parents once again.

Our own grown children, in their thirties,
Are freed up enough to tell us often,
My wife and me, that they love us.
I wish I'd had that freedom back then,
When I was taking my parents' love for granted.
I wish I had not felt so constrained at a time
When I could have put that freedom to good use,
A time when its use would have meant something.

The Bump's Progress

The mother-to-be informs her parents,
First-time grandparents-to-be,
About a website that tracks
The in-the-womb growth of
The baby-to-be,
On line and week-to-week.
They begin to think of it, for short,
As "The Bump-To-Be."

The website, itself called "The Bump,"
Deals in a collection of metaphors,
Takes the interested visitor on
A virtual tour of a supermarket,
A tour helpful to prospective grandparents
Whose years have dulled the memory of
What it was like to await
The arrival of their own offspring.

The tour begins in the spices aisle,
Providing the first standards of measurement.
Two weeks after conception,
The Bump-To-Be is smaller
Than a fleck of ground pepper.
A week later, it has begun to grow,
But is still smaller than a grain of salt.
At five weeks, it is appleseed-sized,
Now to be found in the produce department,
Where its analogues will succeed one another
Until its progress comes to its marvelous end.

At ten weeks, it's as big as a strawberry.
By fifteen weeks, it passes from potency to act,

As a metaphysician might say.
No longer a bump-to-be,
It has produced a real and visible bump,
The size of a navel orange.
At twenty weeks, now banana-sized,
It crosses the half-pregnancy hump
Into the backstretch.
At twenty-five, it is a cauliflower.
At thirty, a zucchini.
At thirty-five, the bump,
Now as large as a pineapple,
Enters the homestretch.

At thirty-nine weeks, its due date arriving,
It is a not-very-big pumpkin,
But it does not remain a pumpkin for long.
As it emerges from its mother's womb and
Enters the world outside,
No longer a nameless bump.
Indeed, it is not even a bump.
It is now a baby girl whose name is Claire,
Seven pounds, five ounces in weight,
Nineteen inches long,
Red of body, wrinkled of face,
Squalling at times but still
Wondrous to behold,
For parents and grandparents alike,
At the end of a supermarket tour.

Vigil

The contractions start on Wednesday,
Contractions preceding real labor.
They continue through the day,
Through the night, into Thursday.

At five on Thursday morning,
The parents-to-be have had enough of waiting.
They take to the road,
Arrive at the hospital by seven,
Alert the doula and the midwife,
Inform the prospective grandparents
By text message, and so
The vigil begins.

Texts from the expectant father
Reach the grandparents-in-waiting
Every few hours –
Brief, positive, undramatic.

The vigil continues into the afternoon.
The husband's mother joins
Her fellow grandparents-to-be for tea
With lemon and a tray of cookies.
All three try to remain calm;
It will be the first grandchild for all.

The brief text messages continue –
Labor progressing, though slowly,
The expectant mother doing well –
But do little to ease the tension affecting
The waiting grandparents-to-be.

As evening approaches,
The husband's mother departs,
His wife's parents left to wait alone.

By seven in the evening,
The labor now twelve hours long,
The anxiety mounts:
How is the baby?
How is the mother?
But the cellphones are quiet and
The parents dare not call,
Knowing their daughter and son-in-law
Have more than enough on their plates.

The grandfather-to-be is afflicted
With unvoiced fear,
Captive to an ancient superstition.
Will a vengeful God punish the baby
For his sins of commission and omission
Over six decades of adult life?

At nine o'clock, fourteen hours
After labor began,
A text from the husband.
The mother-to-be has been given a labor accelerant.
The grandparents wonder what it means.

At eleven, having heard no further word,
The wife's parents decide to retire.
Forty-five minutes later,
They are settling into bed
When the woman's phone buzzes.
She picks up the phone, looks at it, and
Cries out – with alarm, her husband thinks.

He fears the worst, for the baby,
For his daughter, for both.
But no, there was no alarm in that cry.
When his wife holds up the phone,
The screen reveals the scrunched-up face
Of a newborn child, captioned with
A text from the proud father
Inviting his in-laws to welcome
Their granddaughter into the world.
The sixteen-hour vigil comes to an end,
The day's tensions dissolving
In a wave of joy and
Relief and wonder.

ABOUT THE AUTHOR

Born in 1938, Tom grew up in South Philadelphia. He attended St. Joseph's Prep, Philadelphia's Jesuit high school, and the University of Notre Dame, both on academic scholarships. After graduating magna cum laude from Notre Dame in 1960, Tom joined the Jesuits, where he spent most of the next eighteen years. Along the way he was ordained a priest in 1970; acquired graduate degrees in philosophy, English, theology, and law; taught in high school, college, and law school; helped to edit the Jesuit magazine *America*; clerked for a federal judge; and served as staff counsel for a congressional committee investigating the assassination of Dr. Martin Luther King, Jr.

Tom left the Jesuits and the priesthood in 1978. Shortly thereafter he married Ann Dunleavy, having first met her on a blind date when they were college freshmen in 1956. Tom then worked as an attorney in private practice, served as general counsel to a government relations firm, and eventually entered on a seventeen-year career as an appellate attorney in the Criminal Division of the Department of Justice, during which time he argued approximately 65 cases before federal circuit courts of appeals.

Following his retirement from the Department of Justice in 2007, he took a long-delayed plunge into the fine arts, which culminated in a solo 2012 show of 54 paintings and drawings at the Yellow Barn Studio and Gallery in Glen Echo, Maryland. Finally, after writing millions of words of dubious aesthetic value as a journalist and attorney, he began to write poetry seriously in 2013. His first volume of poetry, *Food for a Journey*, received a 2016 Book Excellence Award for Poetry.

Tom and Ann live in Bethesda, Maryland. Their two grown children, Mark and Kate, live in the Washington, D.C. area, where both are attorneys. Kate and her husband, Devin Maroney, have a daughter, Claire, Tom and Ann's first grandchild.

This book is set in Garamond Premier Pro, which had its genesis in 1988 when type-designer Robert Slimbach visited the Plantin-Moretus Museum in Antwerp, Belgium, to study its collection of Claude Garamond's metal punches and typefaces. During the mid-fifteen hundreds, Garamond—a Parisian punch-cutter—produced a refined array of book types that combined an unprecedented degree of balance and elegance, for centuries standing as the pinnacle of beauty and practicality in type-founding. Slimbach has created an entirely new interpretation based on Garamond's designs and on compatible italics cut by Robert Granjon, Garamond's contemporary.

This book is available in all bookstores

•

On the house website
(www.antrimhousebooks.com)
in addition to information on books
you will find sample poems, upcoming events,
and a "seminar room" featuring supplemental biography,
notes, images, poems, reviews, and
writing suggestions.

CPSIA information can be obtained
at www.ICGtesting.com
Printed in the USA
FFHW022254301019
55886889-61759FF

9 781943 826643